# THE BARD
## AND THE BOOK

HOW THE FIRST FOLIO
SAVED THE PLAYS OF
WILLIAM SHAKESPEARE
FROM OBLIVION

### ANN BAUSUM

*Illustrated by*
### MARTA SEVILLA

PEACHTREE
ATLANTA

Published by
**PEACHTREE PUBLISHING COMPANY INC.**
1700 Chattahoochee Avenue
Atlanta, Georgia 30318-2112
*PeachtreeBooks.com*

Design and composition by Kerry Martin
Edited by Catherine Frank

The illustrations were rendered in gouache and colored pencils for the cover,
and digital medium for the inside of the book.

Printed and bound in December 2023 at Toppan Leefung, DongGuan, China.
10 9 8 7 6 5 4 3 2 1
First Edition
978-1-68263-495-0

Library of Congress Cataloging-in-Publication Data

Names: Bausum, Ann, author. | Sevilla, Marta (Illustrator), illustrator.
Title: The bard and the book : how the first folio saved the plays of William Shakespeare
from oblivion / Ann Bausum ; illustrated by Marta Sevilla.
Description: First edition. | Atlanta : Peachtree, 2024. | Includes bibliographical references and index.
Audience: Ages 10 and Up. | Audience: Grades 4–6. | Summary: "The unlikely true story of why we
know the name William Shakespeare today, and the four-hundred-year-old book that made it possible.
Four hundred years ago, no one bothered to write down the exact words of stage plays. Characters' lines
were scribbled on small rolls of paper (as in, an actor's role) and passed around, but no master script was
saved for the future. The main reason we've heard of Romeo, Juliet, Hamlet, and Shakespeare himself
is that a group of people made the excellent choice to preserve the plays after the Bard died. If they
hadn't created the book known as the First Folio, Shakespeare and his works would surely have been
lost to history. Part literary scavenger hunt (the search for every existing First Folio continues today),
part book trivia treasure trove, and part love letter to Shakespeare, this behind-the-scenes, sharply
funny true story is an ideal introduction to the Bard and his famous plays"—Provided by publisher.
Identifiers: LCCN 2023041368 | ISBN 9781682634950 (hardcover) | ISBN 9781682636367 (ebook)
Subjects: LCSH: Shakespeare, William, 1564-1616. Plays. First Folio—Juvenile literature. | Shakespeare,
William, 1564-1616—Juvenile literature. | Early printed books—17th century—Juvenile literature.
Classification: LCC PR3071.B38 2024 | DDC 822.3/3—dc23/eng/20231011
LC record available at https://lccn.loc.gov/2023041368

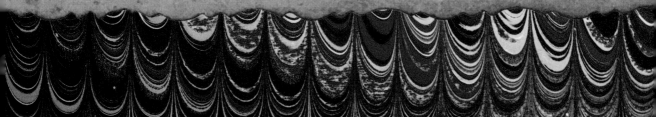

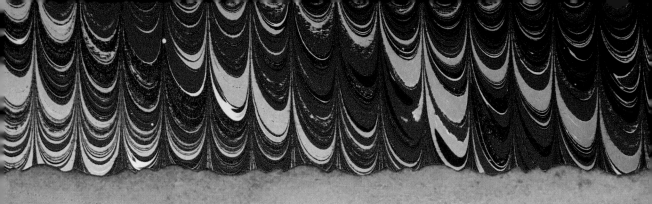

For the Players,
Especially the acting company
at the American Players Theatre
in Spring Green, Wisconsin,
Who keep me laughing, crying,
and joyful.
Bravo!

*Devise, wit; write, pen:*

*for I am for*

*whole*

*volumes*

*in*

*folio.*

## DON ADRIANO DE ARMADO

*Love's Labor's Lost*
ACT I, SCENE 2, LINES 164–165

# CONTENTS

Painting that may be of
William Shakespeare.
Or not. Note earring.

# PROLOGUE

SOMEDAY you may decide that William Shakespeare is unworthy of your attention.

Indeed, perhaps that day has already arrived.

Alas and alack, if so, for you have been misled to think that a dead poet with an earring from more than four hundred years ago has nothing to offer you.

(Actually Shakespeare may not have worn an earring, but some people think he did because of a painting that might be of Shakespeare. Or not. There's a lot we don't know about William Shakespeare, including about that earring. And about the painting, too, for that matter.)

But we are getting ahead of ourselves.

Back to the man and his pen. He definitely had a pen.

Or at least a quill.

There is a reason you will encounter the words of William Shakespeare, willingly or not, in the course of time. Your paths will cross because Shakespeare's words are for the ages. They offer as much meaning in an era of spaceships and digital devices as they did for one of carts and feather pens.

I kid you not.

And someday you may come to agree with me.

As for how Shakespeare's words have survived for more than four hundred years, how it's even possible for you to meet them, that's easy. It all comes down to one book.

A book known the world over by the most generic of titles: The First Folio.

Here is its story.

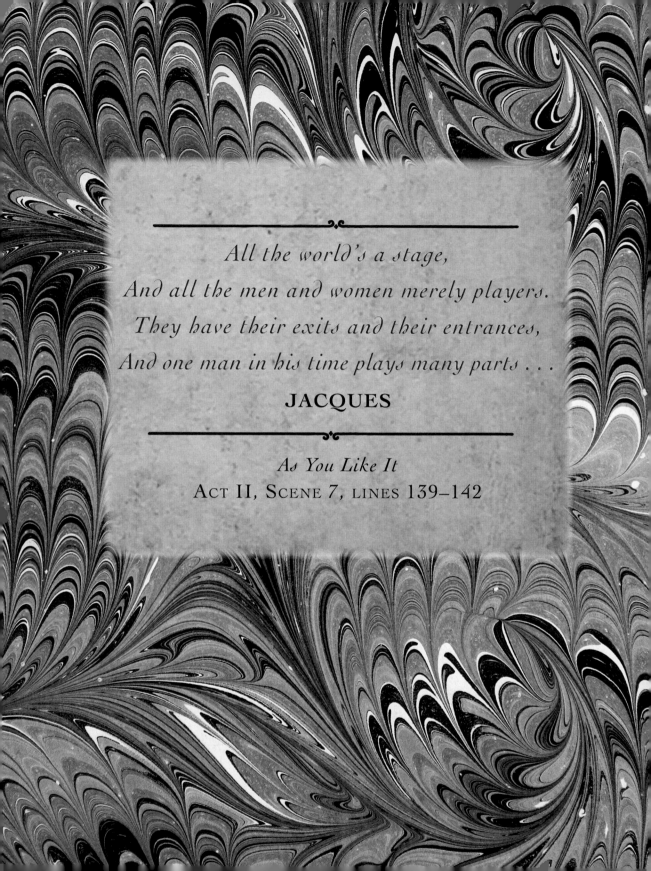

*All the world's a stage,*
*And all the men and women merely players.*
*They have their exits and their entrances,*
*And one man in his time plays many parts . . .*

**JACQUES**

*As You Like It*
ACT II, SCENE 7, LINES 139–142

# ACT I

## WILLIAM SHAKESPEARE BECOMES BRILLIANT, THEN DIES

IN 1564, William Shakespeare made his entrance upon the stage of life in Stratford-upon-Avon, the same English town from which he later took his exit. Some

say his birth and death even fell on the same date, April 23. Some don't, but it's still a nice thought.

Shakespeare's birthplace on the River Avon anchored the arc of his life and inspired an enduring nickname, the Bard of Avon, which means the poet from Avon. But Shakespeare earned his claim to fame in a very different place.

London.

Shakespeare was born here. Well, not here, but in a place that looked a lot like this.

Panorama of London, circa 1625.

Even in the late 1500s it was an astounding city. Its historic center was ringed by the remains of a Roman wall. Commanding stone gates pierced the ancient fortification, and some two hundred thousand people lived within or just beyond its perimeter.

We think William Shakespeare moved to London when he was about twenty-one years old. His wife, Anne, and their children did not. They remained at their family home in Stratford, some one hundred miles north and four or more days away by horse. For most of the next three decades, Shakespeare moved back and forth between these two worlds, but London forever stirred his blood and called him back.

And London filled his purse.

First as an actor.

Then as a playwright.

And eventually as a business partner in a great new theater—the Globe—or, as Shakespeare would later call it: *This wooden O.*

The twenty sides of this almost-circular open-air structure encompassed one of the leading theatrical stages of the day. It competed with such houses as the Rose, the Curtain, and the Swan for an audience hungry to hear the latest works by the astonishing community of playwrights who lived and thrived—and competed with one another—in London.

Christopher Marlowe.

Ben Jonson.

John Fletcher.

Francis Beaumont.

And

William Shakespeare.

Literary scholars spend lifetimes studying famous writers like William Shakespeare. And they have determined that from approximately 1585 to 1613—a span of twenty-eight years—

A cutaway view of the Globe Theater in London.

Shakespeare authored more than three dozen plays. Many were comedies designed to tease and entertain. Some were tragedies full of drama and woe.

Others, the histories, celebrated great tales of English nobility—and helped to keep Shakespeare and his company in the good graces of the Crown. Why? Because the Crown was everything in England in those days, from Queen Elizabeth I to, later on, her distant cousin and successor, King James I. In fact, Shakespeare and his fellow actors so pleased King James that they earned the title of the King's Men and performed in front of him on command at his court. But over time, Shakespeare seems to have acted less and written more. He created the drama; others increasingly portrayed it.

As a playwright, Shakespeare would have used the same tools as his playwriting rivals—paper, ink, and quill pens. To these simple supplies he added his knowledge of history and ancient literature, the stories that sprang from his imagination, and his keen wit. We can only guess what his manuscripts might have looked like because none of them have survived. But the term scholars apply to these lost drafts is the same one the King's Men used for similar scripts as early as 1625:

Foul papers.

And foul they may have been with crossouts, and circles, and arrows, and who knows what else. Food stains? Ink spills? Stray reminders about plans to meet friends that night for dinner? We can ponder the possibilities.

Fortunately for William Shakespeare and the other playwrights of his day, there were theatrical scribes, folks whose job it was to create legible copies of those tangled foul papers. We know that a man named Ralph Crane transcribed a good many of the plays of William Shakespeare. He would have worked word by word and scene by scene until he had produced a clean copy of the playwright's original text.

Then, Crane would have made copies of the actors' parts. To save paper and to keep the play from being stolen by other acting companies, he only wrote down the lines that each player needed to know, their sides, as they're sometimes called. These lines were glued together and then rolled up into individual bundles, one for each part, which the actors would have learned by heart. Those ROLLS of paper were the origin of what we call acting ROLES today.

Shakespeare didn't just write parts willy-nilly in order to tell his story. He wrote them because he knew precisely which actor would help him bring that story to life. Many of today's most celebrated roles were played for the first time by one key member of the King's Men:

Richard Burbage.

Shakespeare wrote the part of Hamlet, but Burbage was the first to portray the young prince tortured by the need to avenge his father's murder.

*To be or not to be: that is the question.*

Actors have probably been asking themselves that same question ever since, measuring their own worth by trying to perform this most challenging of roles. Which makes one wonder: Did Richard Burbage experience similar fear and awe when he first undertook this part?

So many lines!

So many moments onstage!

So many soliloquies (the fancy word for the long speeches that reveal the inner thoughts of a character)!

We'll never know, but we do know he was the first man to play this leading role. And he originated many others.

Shakespeare created the character King Lear, but Burbage wove the playwright's words into the stormy tempest that overtook an aging man who had been betrayed by his oldest daughters.

*Blow wind and crack your cheeks!*

Shakespeare imagined the hunchbacked form of King Richard III on the page, but Burbage transformed his own body on the stage in order to represent a figure misshapen in both body and soul.

*A horse, a horse, my kingdom for a horse!*

There were other leading actors who created famous roles too.

Take Shakespeare's *Henry the Fourth* histories, which are based upon—surprise!—the reign of England's King Henry IV. Shakespeare added the fictional character of Falstaff to enliven the story of the transformation of the king's son, Prince Hal, from a rowdy youth into a future monarch. Audiences went wild for Falstaff, the prince's fun-loving companion, thanks to the spirited performance of a comic actor named William Kemp. All of which was great for Falstaff but less than ideal for Prince Hal, who was supposed to be the main focus of the two-part play, thank you very much!

Some say Shakespeare corrected this imbalance by having the newly crowned king turn on Falstaff at the end of the *Henry the Fourth* series. Then, in the sequel *Henry the Fifth*, he disappears altogether. Audience members who had anticipated seeing fresh Falstaff antics discovered instead that the beloved character had died.

Horrors!

## The Workes of William Shakespeare,

containing all his Comedies, Histories, and Tragedies: Truely set forth, according to their first
*ORIGINALL.*

### The Names of the Principall Actors
in all these Playes.

William Shakespeare.
Richard Burbadge.
John Hemmings.
Augustine Phillips.
William Kempt.
Thomas Poope.
George Bryan.
Henry Condell.
William Slye.
Richard Cowly.
John Lowine.
Samuell Crosse.
Alexander Cooke.

Samuel Gilburne.
Robert Armin.
William Ostler.
Nathan Field.
John Underwood.
Nicholas Tooley.
William Ecclestone.
Joseph Taylor.
Robert Benfield.
Robert Goughe.
Richard Robinson.
John Shancke.
John Rice.

### The Names of the Principall Actors
in all these Playes.

William Shakespeare.
Richard Burbadge.
John Hemmings.
Augustine Phillips.
William Kempt.
Thomas Poope.
George Bryan.
Henry Condell.
William Slye.
Richard Cowly.
John Lowine.
Samuell Crosse.
Alexander Cooke.

Samuel Gilburne.
Robert Armin.
William Ostler.
Nathan Field.
John Underwood.
Nicholas Tooley.
William Ecclestone.
Joseph Taylor.
Robert Benfield.
Robert Goughe.
Richard Robinson.
John Shancke.
John Rice.

A listing of the main actors who performed the plays of William Shakespeare. The letters that almost look like Fs equaled the lowercase letter "s" back in Shakespeare's day.

But (of course) there are competing theories about Falstaff's demise. Others say Shakespeare had to kill him off because the actor who portrayed him had left the company—or maybe he had even been pushed out of it!

Backstage drama is nothing new.

And what about the leading ladies?

Well, there were none.

That's because women were forbidden from taking to the stage.

At all.

Yes, you read that correctly.

(Shakespeare had been dead for more than forty years before this ban was lifted.)

There's a reason Shakespeare and his fellow actors were called the King's MEN. In his company, and in all others at that time in England, the heroines were performed by teens and young men up to the age of about twenty-one. These actors had voices that could project higher tones, and their appearances could be disguised to look feminine.

This system actually worked pretty well.

When costumed and wigged, a youth could convincingly portray Juliet in Shakespeare's tragic story of her love with Romeo.

*Parting is such sweet sorrow.*

Or a teenage boy could amuse the audience by portraying a female character who was in turn pretending to be a man.

*Were it not better*
*Because that I am more than common tall,*
*That I did suit me all points like a man.*

All of which was endlessly entertaining, and well and good.

BUT there is this thing called aging, and Shakespeare wasn't getting any younger, particularly by the standards of the day. In the year 1610, or thereabouts, he took up residence again in his hometown. Shakespeare was in his late forties by then, and had become a grandfather. He seems to have planned to spend more time with his family and less time in London, even if he did continue to write.

Long before the decade was out, though, his life had ended. No one made a record of how he died— or those notes haven't survived if they did—but he appears to have had a brief illness at age fifty-two or so. One story emerged later on claiming that he had gone out drinking with visiting friends, including the playwright Ben Jonson, and become ill with a fever that led to his death.

Maybe that happened.

Or maybe not.

It's like the earring in that portrait. There is so much we will never know for sure.

Even the date of Shakespeare's death is subject to some debate, although most folks go with April 23, 1616, noting that he was buried two days later, on April 25.

Alas and alack!

One thing was sure. There would be no new plays. And the man who knew all the old favorites so intimately was no longer there to help keep them alive.

The Bard of Avon was dead.

William Shakespeare, as portrayed on a funerary monument near his grave in Stratford-upon-Avon.

*If it live in your memory,*

*begin at this line . . .*

**HAMLET**

TO THE PLAYER KING

*Hamlet*
ACT II, SCENE 2, LINES 370–371

# ACT II

## THE FLEETING NATURE OF THEATER PREPARES TO VANQUISH MACBETH

WHEN Richard Burbage created the role of Macbeth in something like 1606, he studied his roll of text, committed the villain's lines to

memory, and repeated them with passions drawn from his heart. That was how the theater worked.

Playwrights wrote. Actors memorized. And companies competed for audiences to attend their productions. The lines of a play lived in the memories of the people who performed and watched them. Paper rolls might or might not survive, and only occasionally would a script find its way into print. When one did, it really wasn't the playwright's business. Literally.

At that time, publishers could reproduce plays without the author's permission and without paying them any compensation for their work. Theaters owned these scripts, not their authors. Playwrights wrote to have their words performed, not to see them printed. Even so, Shakespeare's plays were popular enough for eighteen of them to have found their way into print during his lifetime. These thin books were and are known as the quartos, and the reason why is simple. Each one was printed on a sheet of paper that was folded . . .

Once.

And once more.

Until one sheet of paper had become one-fourth, or one quarter, of its original size.

Quarter.

Quarto.

When the short folds of that sheet were cut apart, that single piece of paper yielded four quarter-sized pages that, having been printed on both sides, became eight pages in a book.

If you wanted an even smaller publication, you could follow the same process but fold the bundle an additional time. This method resulted in pages that were an eighth of the sheet's original size, which yielded an equally straightforward name.

Octavo.

Shakespeare undoubtedly knew about the quarto editions of his plays, but he is unlikely to have helped to make them, because, as previously noted, it was none of his business. Some of the printed editions captured his language quite accurately, but others did not. At least, that's what literary scholars concluded during the twentieth century. Indeed, they viewed several editions as so seemingly inferior that they gave them a special name:

The bad quartos.

Depending on how one defines "bad," there are at least four of them, with an early printing of *Hamlet* being famously out of sync with other versions of the play. (Just so you know, when it's not being called the bad quarto, this 1603 publication is called the First Quarto of *Hamlet*.) More recently scholars have proposed that the bad quartos may not be so bad after all; they're just shorter—short quartos, they're sometimes called—offering different versions of the same play.

Let us consider this suggestion. Take that First Quarto of *Hamlet*. It offers a twist on one of the most famous lines Shakespeare ever wrote. In it Hamlet proclaims:

*"To be, or not to be—ay, there's the point."*

But, no. That is not the point. Not the point at all.

The point is: Could the First Quarto version have endured for centuries? Let us hope not. For the world is in love with the line that goes:

*To be or not to be: that is the question.*

The fact that we know this line is partly due to the publication a year or so later of a better quarto of *Hamlet*—Whew!—which not surprisingly is known as the Second Quarto.

As for Shakespeare, he and the King's Men were performing his words at the Globe and at court, and they

*THE*
Tragicall Historie of
H A M L E T,
*Prince of Denmarke.*

By William Shakespeare.

Newly imprinted and enlarged to almost as much againe as it was, according to the true and perfect Coppie.

AT LONDON,
Printed by I. R. for N. L. and are to be sold at his shoppe vnder Saint Dunstons Church in Fleetstreet. 1604.

The title page for the Second Quarto edition of *Hamlet*, published 1604.

were getting along just fine, thank you very much. At least they were doing fine so long as the bubonic plague stayed away, which it did enough years for them to survive, and even thrive.

But then their hearts began to give out.

Shakespeare's in 1616.

Richard Burbage's in 1619.

And with the hearts went the lines that had lived for years in the minds of Shakespeare and his fellow players.

Lines that were growing fainter,

and fainter,

and fainter,

like the heartbeats of each player.

So faint, in fact, that they were at risk of vanishing into OBLIVION, that place where countless other plays have gone to die.

There's a reason young people study the plays of William Shakespeare instead of those by his contemporaries John Fletcher and Francis Beaumont. Shakespeare's plays survived; theirs were largely lost.

And why did his survive?

They survived because someone thought about his plays soon after his death and had A BIG IDEA.

We can argue over who had it first—and literary scholars DO argue about this and much else—but let us agree that it was good SOMEONE had it because otherwise we probably would have lost HALF the plays of William Shakespeare, plays such as

*The Tempest*
and
*The Comedy of Errors*
and
*gasp*
*Macbeth.*
*Double, double, toil and trouble; Fire burn and cauldron bubble.*

Maybe the BIG IDEA started with Shakespeare's friends, people like John Heminge and Henry Condell who had acted with him and been among his business partners at the Globe. Or maybe it started with William and Isaac Jaggard, a father and son with a family printing business in London.

In any case, the idea ARRIVED. The revolutionary idea that plays—at least the plays of William Shakespeare—were worth preserving, that they were too good to be FORGOTTEN, that they should endure

       beyond

            living

                 memory.

This was a radical suggestion.

For thousands of years, texts had survived in people's heads more easily than on paper. Paper was time-consuming to make, and that made it expensive to buy. Each sheet was formed one leaf at a time, by hand, and when words were deemed worthy of being preserved on paper, each sheet was filled one word at a time, by hand.

About one hundred years before Shakespeare's birth, this tradition of hand-copied texts met a formidable challenger:

The printing press.

A German named Johannes Gutenberg had invented the first mechanical press around 1440. By the time Shakespeare's words were entertaining the people of

London, presses were thumping throughout the city. Some of them were even printing copies of Shakespeare's plays and those of other London playwrights. But paper was still expensive, and printers preferred to reproduce more serious works—such as the Bible—or more practical material—such as legal notices. The theater was widely seen as a form of fleeting, frivolous entertainment, not as literature to be read and reread on a page.

Yes, there were the quartos, but these were the exceptions. Ben Jonson, one of Shakespeare's contemporaries, helped to change all that. When this celebrated author published his collected *Workes* in 1616, he didn't just include his famous poems; he added his plays. This was a daring move, and Jonson's boldness

An early printing press.

shocked his readers. Poetry was considered a true work of art. Plays, not so much. Critics joked that he had made a mistake by confusing "play" with "work."

*Pray tell me Ben, where doth the mystery lurke*
*What others call a play you call a worke.*

NEVERTHELESS, Heminge and Condell, plus the Jaggards and a few other printers and publishers, including one named Edward Blount, decided to follow Ben Jonson's lead and do it one better. They were determined to make what would become the FIRST collection EVER printed that was ENTIRELY filled with PLAYS, the plays of William Shakespeare.

As they made their plans they thought

# BIG.

They thought bigger than octavos.
They thought bigger than quartos.
They thought all the way to the biggest book of all:

# THE FOLIO.

At that time every sheet of paper was made using wooden frames that were filled with a slurry of boiled fibers. In fact, papermaking was an early form of recycling—the end product of a process that started with worn-out clothes and cast-off linens. (There's a reason it was called rag paper.)

The frames that held this paper soup could only be so big.

How big?

Folio-big.

And folio-big was pretty big. Each folio-sized sheet of paper was about as large as a fully opened laptop, or about eighteen inches wide and fourteen inches tall. When a sheet of paper was folded in half, it was as if one had shut a laptop, reducing the width by half but leaving the sheet just as tall. Like this:

Making a sheet of paper.

This folded sheet created four surfaces—aka four pages in a book.

There was more than one reason to fold the leaf of folio-sized paper in half. Not only did it make four distinct pages, but the hinge where it folded was useful too.

When it came time to assemble each book:

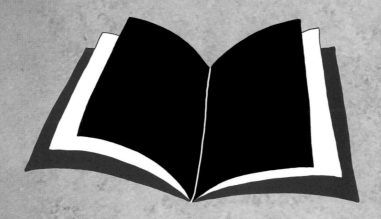

One sheet could be tucked around another sheet and around another sheet . . .

Until you had three sheets of folio paper and—do the math—twelve pages of text. This tidy bundle could then be bound together by a thread that was sewn along its hinged fold.

These gathered sheets were known as a quire (pronounced like "choir"—don't ask; that's just the way it is). So, start with one quire, and add another quire . . .

And another.

And another, and another, and another, and another, and another, and another, and another, and another, and another.

And ANOTHER.

And you begin to have a book.

Okay, maybe it hasn't crossed your mind yet, but you should consider how tricky it would have been to keep one quire straight from the next.

What about page numbers? you ask.

Yes, what about page numbers?

Alas, page numbers weren't particularly helpful.

In fact, they weren't helpful at all.

With big projects like this one—projects where

different parts of the book were in production at the same time—it was nearly impossible to accurately predict sequential page numbering for an entire publication. Indeed, if someone asked you to start reading on page one of what became the first collection of Shakespeare's plays, you would have several choices of where to begin.

Of course the first play in the book, *The Tempest*, conveniently starts on page one. So do the plays that kick off the histories and the tragedies, for that matter. Which sort of makes sense, right? But even so there are plenty of breaks and gaps in the sequencing within these sections.

Take *The Comedy of Errors*, which has two page 88s nestled around page 87 but no page 86 in sight. Definitely not as funny as all the errors that unfold in the play, but, still, the pagination is its own comedy of errors.

Or consider *The Tragedy of Troilus and Cressida*—which for reasons that aren't entirely clear—made it into most copies of the print run but not all of them. As for its page numbers? Well, it practically has no page numbers at all.

So forget about page numbers. They were worthless.

Instead, publishers used a different method that was more compatible with the era's system of printing. It all came back to the quires. As the printers worked, they assigned each quire a printed code—called a signature—that appeared in a corner on every sheet and showed that its pages belonged together. No page numbers required. Signatures ran through the alphabet (A1 being the obvious place to start) and then repeated the alphabet again. And again. And again, quire after quire, until the printing was done, perhaps ending with, say, bbb12. (We're not talking rocket science here.)

And how did they put the signatures in order later on?

One trick they used was the catchword. The catchword appeared in the bottom right corner of every page. It previewed the next word in the text, the one that would appear at the top of the following page. Confused? Let's try it right now. This paragraph is nearly done. In fact, it will be done when we read the word "goes." And that word will be followed on the next page by "Did," so we will use "Did" as our catchword after we conclude this paragraph. Here goes.

Did

Did you see how that worked? Kinda nifty, right? The catchword assured that someone printed the right text on the back side of the previous page. And it helped to match up the endings and beginnings of all those quires.

BUT

We are getting ahead of ourselves.

Again.

How could Heminge and Condell and the Jaggards and Blount and others collect the plays of William Shakespeare if the people who knew his words had died?

A spread from the First Folio showing the end of *All's Well that Ends Well* and the beginning of *Twelfth Night*. Enlarged detail of the bottom right corner shows the signature (Y2) and catchword (Till) for page 255.

A glooming peace this morning with it brings;
The sun for sorrow will not show his head.

**PRINCE**

*Romeo and Juliet*
Act V, Scene 3, lines 305–306

# ACT III

## ROMEO AND JULIET TUSSLE WITH THEIR FIRST TEEN READER

FORTUNATELY, not everyone was dead yet. Take Heminge and Condell. They had acted in supporting roles in Shakespeare's plays for years and would have heard the leading

parts often enough to have many of those lines in their heads too.

And there were the quartos—the good quartos—fourteen of them.

As for the bad quartos (or the short quartos), well, forget about them.

They were no help at all.

FORTUNATELY thanks to Heminge and Condell and other King's Men, there were prompt books.

Prompt books were the copies of the plays that were used to help actors during rehearsals—to PROMPT them when they needed to be reminded of a line. Prompt books showed the texts of the plays, but they held other useful details too.

Who should walk onto the stage—make an entrance.

Who else should be onstage, even if they never spoke any lines.

When someone should exit the stage.

Even when someone should exit the stage "pursued by a bear."

*(Yes, it really says that. See Act III, Scene 3 of The Winter's Tale.)*

And FORTUNATELY Ralph Crane's heart continued to beat, so he was around to help. Ralph Crane had copied so many plays by William Shakespeare that he would have been an extremely useful collaborator. There were other potential resources too. Remember Shakespeare's foul papers? Maybe some of those still existed and could be consulted during the production process. Ditto for rolls, those copies of individual speaking parts.

So with good quartos, and prompt books, and perhaps even rolls and foul papers, the people who best knew Shakespeare's words assembled the texts of each play. Because they anticipated that the scripts were going to be read, they often divided the scenes of the original texts into acts, five of them, introducing natural breaks that hadn't been needed initially on a stage. These acts worked like chapters to enhance the reading experience. The acts didn't have to be the same length; they just had to bring order to the text, rather like the acts that are used to organize this book.

And THEN the staff at Jaggard's printing house went to work.

This

work

took

time.

And it took letters, lots and lots of letters. Letters that had been cast out of lead to form their individual shapes. So many letters that there were boxes full of them. That's because every letter of every word had to be assembled by hand before a page could be printed . . .

L-e-t-t-e-r

by

l-e-t-t-e-r

and

space by space.

Oh, and in BACKWARD order.

Yes, **ꓭꓱAWꓘƆAꓭ**!

Because that was the only way to make the letters come out frontward when they were printed:

# BACKWARD.

That was how printing worked. It didn't matter if you were creating an octavo edition, a quarto, or a folio. Everyone followed the same system.

The people who COMPOSED these backward words were called, logically, COMPOSITORS. Each compositor would assemble sections of text letter by letter using what was called a composing stick. Then they

Composing stick.

painstakingly transferred these blocks of type to a frame, known as the galley. After a galley had been filled, it was secured in place on the printing press and coated with ink. Next, a sheet of damp paper (all of which had been imported from France, by the way) was aligned upon this printing bed. Then the whole assembly, called a carriage, was rolled under the weight-bearing tower of the printing press. After the carriage was in place, the press operator would manually apply pressure to the assembly, leaving a clear impression of the inked letters on the sheet.

Voilà!

When the sheet came off the press, all that backward type had become readable, and you'd made one page of a book. Then that sheet of paper got hung up to dry, and the process was repeated.

More ink. More paper.

More ink. More paper.

More ink. More paper.

Until all the required copies of a page had been printed. Then it was time for the next page in the book.

It took about three hundred years for literary scholars to figure out how the book's composition had been done,

Hanging printed pages to dry.

with particular thanks due to Charlton Hinman for his work on this puzzle during the twentieth century. Over time, Hinman and others determined that as many as nine people composed the type for the collected plays of William Shakespeare. And what was their biggest clue? SPELLING.

The rules of spelling were pretty casual when Shakespeare's plays were being prepared for printing.

The process of printing, from composing
type to inking and printing it.

Someone, who for lack of a better name is known as
Compositor A, liked to spell certain words one way:

*doe,*

*goe,*

*here*.

And a person identified as Compositor B spelled the
same words differently:

*do,*

*go,*

*heere.*

Each person spelled differently, but each compositor spelled consistently, and for good reason.

Remember those boxes filled with letters?

Each compositor worked from their own pair of wooden boxes. The two cases of letters were sloped so that their contents could be easily seen, and they were stacked one directly behind the other for convenient arm's-reach access. The upper case held what were called majuscule letters. (Think capital letters.) The lower case held the corresponding smaller letters, which at that time were called minuscule letters.

Each case was divided into compartments, and each compartment held multiple copies of the same letter. There were twenty-five compartments for letters ("X" hadn't come into use yet), and dozens of additional compartments for punctuation marks and other symbols. Today, when we refer to letters as being uppercase and lowercase, we are using names that originated with these storage containers.

Some things don't change.

Compositors memorized the location of every letter in their cases the same way we memorize the placement of the alphabet on a keyboard. As they worked, they read a manuscript with their eyes while their hands selected the corresponding (backward) letters. Each compositor spelled consistently because, well, that's how they spelled—AND because they knew what would happen next. After all the copies of a page had been printed, the compositor would have to distribute the type back into their boxes, which meant they had to dismantle it and return the individual letters to their designated upper- and lowercase compartments.

L-e-t-t-e-r

by

l-e-t-t-e-r.

If compositors spelled consistently, they would be able to distribute their type more quickly and accurately. Then they'd be ready to compose again and could trust that their fingers were finding the correct letters of type. All of which helps to explain how scholars figured out the existence of Compositor A and Compositor B. And Compositors C and D, too, for that matter.

Which brings us to Compositor E.

We don't know the names of most of the people who worked for William and Isaac Jaggard, but scholars do think we know the name of Compositor E. He was John Leason, a youth of some seventeen years' age. This young man became an apprentice at the printing house on November 8, 1622, while Shakespeare's plays were being composed. As an apprentice, he would have worked for minimal compensation—probably nothing more than a place to sleep, food, and clothing. In exchange he learned a new trade, or skill, which in John Leason's case appears to have been composition.

The reason scholars associate the work of Compositor E with John Leason is simple. Compositor E's work was

not

very

good.

Compositor E made mistakes.

Lots of mistakes.

So many mistakes that the work seems almost certain to have been done by someone still learning the tedious and exacting craft of composition.

There's a reason we have the expression "mind your p's and q's." That advice was created for people like John

Leason. If John Leason wasn't careful, he might forget that the compositor's letters for "p" and "q" had to be judged in reverse. The letter shaped like a "p" would actually print as a "q"; the shape of "q" made a "p."

# q    p

It was tricky enough when composing, and trickier still when it came time to distribute previously used letters back into their proper places in the cases. Anyone new to the job was bound to make mistakes. And John Leason made plenty of them.

Appropriately enough, the teenage Leason composed the lines for the doomed teen couple in *Romeo and Juliet*, among other plays. Scholars figured this out by studying multiple versions of the same pages from different printed copies of Shakespeare's collected plays. Unlike books today, variations frequently existed between these pages. The same act, the same scene, the same lines might appear on the paper, but they might not match perfectly.

And for good reason.

Remember how time-consuming and expensive it was to make paper? Errors, when—and if—they were caught, were spotted by someone reviewing the pages as a sort of proofreader. This person might mark the error on the sheet and then get the type corrected before further copies of it were printed. Books still have proofreaders. THIS book had a proofreader. But back then, rather than throw out a perfectly good sheet of paper, hand-corrected pages found their way into bound books, mistakes and all. For that matter, sheets with uncorrected errors would show up in bound books too.

It was all a bit random, truthfully.

Take *Othello*, which John Leason also helped to compose. Some copies might begin a song from Act IV of the play with the line:

*The poore Sonle set sining, by a Sicamour tree.*

Even for someone used to variations in seventeenth-century spelling, this was an admittedly unhelpful version of the actual verse:

*The poore Soule sat singing, by a Sicamour tree.*

Both versions made it into print.

Scholars have calculated that compositors had to set (and distribute) some four million pieces of type to prepare the first-ever collection of Shakespeare's plays. The entire process of composing and printing the book took nearly two years, including the final step of organizing the quires—in signature order!—so that they could be sold to buyers.

By November of 1623, seven years after Shakespeare's death, the work was done. Then John Heminge, and Henry Condell, and Edward Blount, and Isaac Jaggard (but not William; he had died along the way) did what all publishers do after completing a book.

They waited to see if anyone would buy it.

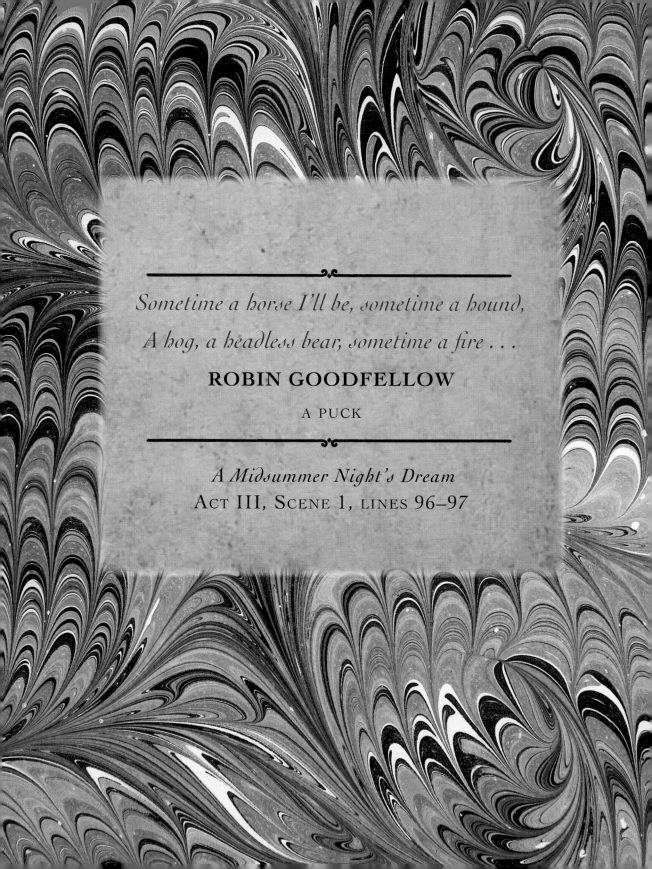

*Sometime a horse I'll be, sometime a hound,*
*A hog, a headless bear, sometime a fire . . .*

## ROBIN GOODFELLOW

A PUCK

*A Midsummer Night's Dream*
ACT III, SCENE 1, LINES 96–97

# ACT IV

## SHAKESPEARE CATCHES FIRE, LITERALLY

AMAZINGLY, we think we know who purchased the first copy of the new book. His name was Sir Edward Dering, and even if this twenty-five-year-old

Sir Edward Dering.

gentleman from Kent didn't buy the VERY first copy, he bought ONE of the first. Or at least he is the first person we know of who bought a copy after it went on sale at the bookseller stalls in the churchyard of St. Paul's Cathedral in London.

Dering made his purchase on December 5, 1623.

We know this fact because he made a note of the expense in his daily accounting records. In fact, based on the amount of money that he spent, which was £2, it appears that he didn't just purchase one copy of the newly collected plays of William Shakespeare.

He bought two.

(Dering was a well-documented book lover and theater enthusiast.)

Literary scholars have speculated for some time about the number of copies that might have been printed of the 1623 edition of Shakespeare's plays. No one knows for sure—there are no surviving records to tell us—

but most people agree that a good guess is 750 copies.

It might surprise you to know that those copies left Jaggard's printing house without any covers. That's because printers didn't bind books.

Bookbinders did.

And they did so uniquely.

The idea that all copies of the same book would appear identical never crossed anyone's mind in 1623. Indeed, it would have seemed absurd. That's because back then the appearance of someone's books was as per-sonalized as their clothing—a statement of tastes, and preferences, and wealth—and it was the bookbinder's job to dress the books.

Maybe all the volumes in a library had matching red leather covers. Or brown ones. Or were tooled (as in carved) with distinct patterns and flourishes. Or were made from sheepskin. Or calfskin.

Who knew what someone would want?

A bookbinder at work.

The customer knew, of course. Because even then, seemingly, the customer was always right.

All of which suggests you shouldn't believe it when you're told that you can't judge a book by its cover.

Unlike books printed today, including this book, those customized covers helped to make each copy distinctive in that 1623 edition. So did the pages found inside. Remember all those variations in composing? Literary scholars began to hunt for them and for other discrepancies between copies as a way to learn more about the book's text and its printing process. Over time they have identified hundreds, indeed thousands, of distinct features that act almost like fingerprints to make each copy UNIQUE.

During the four centuries since their publication, these individual copies have taken on individual identities, each one separate from the next. They have acquired distinct personalities, reputations, and values. Because each copy is different and each copy has its own history, many of them have earned their own names. Collectors and scholars memorize these names the way we learn a family tree, and they talk about individual books the way we discuss our family members.

There are, for example:

The Vincent Folio

and

The Stevens Folio

and

The Golden Retriever Folio.

Yes.

The Golden Retriever Folio.

Like the dog.

That's because this copy had at one time been owned by Dudley Coutts Marjoribanks (whose last name is reportedly, and rather surprisingly, pronounced "Marchbanks," and who eventually earned the title of the first Baron Tweedmouth).

But never mind that.

The key fact is that in 1868, he established the golden retriever breed by crossing a rare gold-colored sporting dog named Nous with a Tweed Water Spaniel called Belle. Three golden retriever puppies followed—Cowslip, Crocus, and Primrose. Even more important is the fact that those pups provide an unexpected way to remember the particularly notable point that the baron owned a copy of the 1623 publication.

Copies of the original edition of Shakespeare's collected plays haven't just earned particular names. Scholars assign them characteristics, too: of being notably tall (that would be the Vincent Folio), or particularly soiled (Shakespearean scholar Samuel Johnson apparently liked to read while eating), or sadly incomplete (the copy that at one time belonged to someone named George Gwynn), or remarkably perfect (the Grenville Folio), or especially pungent.

Yes, pungent.

As in it had a strong smell.

This notable volume was acquired in the nineteenth century by an American collector named Thomas Pennant Barton. But, just so you know, this book is not always identified as the Barton Folio. Some people lovingly describe it as the Farting Folio. That's because when it is cracked open its pages exude hefty hints of barnyard odor, perhaps the result of an unfortunate storage decision. Or maybe the smell is the consequence of faulty preparation of the hide that became the book's leather cover, a process that sometimes involved the use of animal dung. (After Barton's death, the Farting Folio and all Barton's other Shakespeariana were acquired by the Boston Public Library, and that's where the book remains. Smells and all.)

Of course no one called their copies the Farting Folio or the Vincent Folio or the Golden Retriever Folio when they started buying them in 1623. They called them by the book's title, thank you very much, which was:

*Mr. William Shakespeare's Comedies, Histories, and Tragedies, Published according to the True Originall Copies.*

(Yes, that's how they spelled "original.")

This fact was made abundantly clear when the book went on sale:

The title page for the First Folio. The illustration of Shakespeare was engraved by an artist named Martin Droeshout.

Later the volume earned a shorter title, the one we use today: The FIRST Folio.

As the name suggests, this was not the only folio-sized collection of Shakespeare's plays. Subsequent editions eventually earned the predictable names of

The Second Folio (1632)

The Third Folio (1663)

And the Fourth Folio (1685).

Newer was not always better.

Today the most coveted edition of the four is the original edition. The First Folio has historical significance because it was first, obviously, but it's also considered the most complete and authentic of the four books. It was created by people who had known Shakespeare and who were drawing from their living memories of him and his plays. Subsequent editions included dramatic works that scholars have concluded were not authored by Shakespeare, and they introduced errors that had not existed in the First Folio.

The First Folio is not, however, the rarest of the four volumes; more copies of it have survived than of the Third Folio, for example. (See next page.) Even so, most First Folios are gone. Some copies may have vanished early on, discarded following a rule of thumb still employed by the librarians who manage collections of books:

When a new edition appears, it should take the place of the old one.

Countless copies of the first three Shakespeare collections were lost in 1666 during the Great Fire of London. Some would have perished at individual addresses; others went up in flames alongside the other titles held by the booksellers in the churchyard at

An illustration of the Great Fire of London, 1666.

St. Paul's Cathedral. (The recently published Third Folio was particularly hard-hit by this calamitous fire, which helps to account for its rarity.)

Other copies of the First Folio were likely consumed in less famous blazes, or damaged by water, or nibbled by mice, or, well, your guess is as good as mine. There are lots of ways to ruin a book over the course of hundreds of years.

Pages from one copy of the First Folio were known to have been repurposed to wrap fish. Pages from damaged or incomplete copies were cannibalized to fill in the gaps that had developed in different copies. Perhaps other fragments were used to kindle fires, or mop up kitchen spills, or fill drafty cracks under doors.

Seriously, there are lots of ways to ruin an old book.

*Oh, wonderful, wonderful, and most wonderful—wonderful and yet again wonderful, and after that out of all hooping!*

**CELIA**

*As You Like It*
ACT III, SCENE 2, LINES 175–177

# ACT V

## THE WORLD GOES NUTS FOR SHAKESPEARE

**A**ROUND the turn of the previous century, a British scholar named Sidney Lee embarked on a quest to identify all the surviving copies of the

First Folio. By 1902 he had found 158 of them. Then he kept looking and discovered 14 more.

People have been tracking down copies of the First Folio ever since. In 1990, Anthony James West, a former business consultant, decided to improve on Lee's work. He was determined to make the most comprehensive inventory possible of the famed edition.

He is still at it.

By 2012, West and additional colleagues, including literary scholar Eric Rasmussen, had meticulously documented 232 copies of the book. Two years later they confirmed the discovery of a previously unidentified First Folio; this one had come to light among a collection of rare books at a public library in France. Then, in 2016, two more copies emerged. The first had been resting without fanfare for more than two centuries in a private collection in Warwickshire, about twenty miles from Shakespeare's birthplace. The second turned up unexpectedly in the library of a grand estate on a Scottish island. Stay tuned. There could be more.

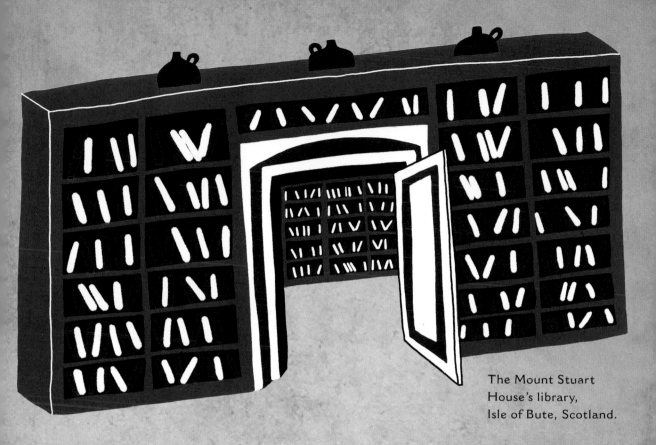

The Mount Stuart
House's library,
Isle of Bute, Scotland.

West's team aims not just to identify every known copy of the First Folio but also to make note of every unique detail of every single page of each book.

The typos.

The nature of its binding.

The watermarks embedded in its sheets of paper that show where the paper was made.

Every written comment on a volume's pages. The doodles added by a child who drew in the margins of the Hacket Folio.

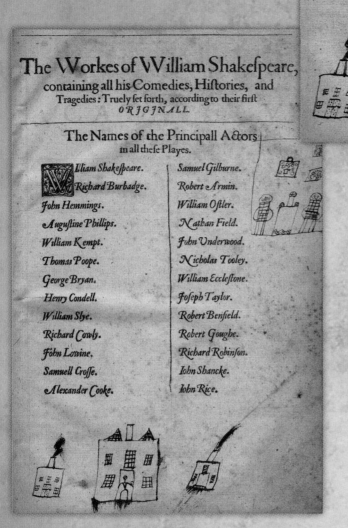

The Workes of William Shakespeare, containing all his Comedies, Histories, and Tragedies: Truely set forth, according to their first ORIGINALL.

The Names of the Principall Actors in all these Playes.

William Shakespeare.
Richard Burbadge.
John Hemmings.
Augustine Phillips.
William Kempt.
Thomas Poope.
George Bryan.
Henry Condell.
William Slye.
Richard Cowly.
John Lowine.
Samuell Grosse.
Alexander Cooke.

Samuel Gilburne.
Robert Armin.
William Ostler.
Nathan Field.
John Underwood.
Nicholas Tooley.
William Ecclestone.
Joseph Taylor.
Robert Benfield.
Robert Goughe.
Richard Robinson.
Iohn Shancke.
Iohn Rice.

The Hacket Folio, enhanced with unexpected illustrations (left, and enlarged detail, above). Much fun was clearly had. The punishment that likely followed, not so much.

The rusty imprint of a pair of scissors at the opening of Act III of *The Merry Wives of Windsor* in the Fitzherbert Folio. The so-called Purple Copy, which has—you guessed it—some pages that trend toward shades of purple.

And more.

Why bother? I hear you ask.

Why bother?! Because that's what people do who share a passion for something, whether it's understanding a work of literature, or studying a feature of the natural world, or figuring out how to visit a distant planet. Such pursuits challenge our minds and fill our hearts with wonder. That's certainly true for the folks who choose to study—some would say obsess about—one of the most famous books of all time.

No one knows when this work will be complete. And, frankly, could it ever be? Because, of course, no one knows where a First Folio might be hiding.

Forgotten in an ancient attic.

Secretly held by a loving collector.

Misshelved in a cavernous library.

Misidentified as one of the later editions.

The possibilities are endless.

What we do know is the whereabouts of 235 copies. And we know that an amazing number of them—more than a third of them, in fact, or 82 copies to be precise—are in one place:

Washington, DC.

That eighty-two copies of the First Folio would have found their way to a location more than three thousand miles from their home country of England is a story in and of itself.

BRIEFLY, it is the story of two people.

Henry Clay Folger and Emily Jordan Folger.

This married couple adored not only each other but also Shakespeare and the First Folio. During their lifetimes they amassed what was then (and arguably still is) the most remarkable collection ever of all things Shakespeare. Before they died they arranged for these materials to be preserved for scholarly study in a building which they commissioned expressly for that purpose:

The Folger Shakespeare Library.

This facility opened to great fanfare within sight of the Capitol in 1932.

Why Washington, DC? you may ask.

That is a good question.

The Folgers lived in New York City, and they would gladly have established their library there. But land was expensive in Manhattan. Too expensive. So instead Henry and Emily latched onto the idea of locating their

The main Reading Room at the Folger Shakespeare Library, Washington, DC.

collection in Washington, DC, where it could be appreciated as a national treasure.

Today, scholars travel from all over the world to study at the Folger. Some stay for months, or longer. Others, including yours truly, are equally thrilled to make shorter visits. There is much to see: a wealth of material about the period when Shakespeare lived, 260,000 related books (including eleven copies of Ben Jonson's *Workes*), and tens of thousands of manuscripts, pieces of art, and other artifacts.

Most notably, the Folger Shakespeare Library is home to the Vincent Folio, the Golden Retriever Folio, and eighty more uniquely bound copies of the FIRST Folio.

Very few people possess their own copy of this book any longer; just twenty-seven are estimated to be held in private hands. The First Folio has become an expensive commodity, often selling for millions of dollars, and few people have the means to purchase and safeguard such a valuable possession. Today, most copies are held by institutions like libraries, and museums, and universities at various spots around the world. In fact, five of the seven continents are home to First Folios; only Antarctica and South America lack one.

We know that 82 of the world's 235 First Folios live at the Folger, but where else do they reside? There's always that Farting Folio in Boston, of course. Or the other 65 copies located around the United States. Or the 50 copies that remain in the United Kingdom, including 5 owned by the British Museum in London. Or the 3 that have settled in Stratford-upon-Avon. Or the 10 copies held in Tokyo, at Meisei University.

Et cetera, et cetera.

These volumes represent the first pages collected sheet by sheet from presses that printed letters arranged one at a time—backward!—to form words that had emerged years earlier from the ink-dipped quill pen of the Bard of Avon.

No matter who you are or where you live, the contents of this most miraculous of books live on for all of us to enjoy. Multiple copies have been digitized and can be viewed online at any time. And you don't have to ever see a First Folio to meet the villainous Macbeth, or to be bewitched by fairies in *A Midsummer Night's Dream*, or to swoon at the passion of "Juliet and her Romeo."

You can savor those stories—and hear Hamlet's immortal speech about that most important of all questions, "To be or not to be"—because they've been preserved

and studied

and memorized

and performed

and loathed

and LOVED

for such a very long time.

All thanks to one book.

The First Folio of the plays of William Shakespeare, Bard of Avon.

# EPILOGUE

**F**EW authors become immortal, their words cherished through the ages, but William Shakespeare, that Bard of Avon, is one of them, thanks in large part to the First Folio.

So take a bow, John Heminge:

And Henry Condell:

And Edward Blount:

**And William and Isaac Jaggard:**

And all the others who dared to make a book.

Bravo, one and all! With their help, William Shakespeare's words are still known by heart.

That is a good thing.

Equally pleasing is the knowledge that these words, which have endured for more than four hundred years, seem destined to survive for hundreds more.

In our hearts.

In our heads.

On stages.

And on the pages of First Folios all around the globe.

Play on!

O thou monster, Ignorance, how deformed
dost thou look!

**HOLOFERNES**

. . .

Sir, he hath never fed of the dainties
that are bred in a book.
He hath not eat paper, as it were;
he hath not drunk ink.
His intellect is not replenished . . .

**NATHANIEL**

*Love's Labor's Lost*
ACT IV, SCENE 2, LINES 20–23

# CONTENTS OF THE FIRST FOLIO

Categorized according to the genres assigned at the time of publication in 1623; titles are listed in the order presented in the First Folio.

## COMEDIES

The Tempest[+]

The Two Gentlemen of Verona[+]

The Merry Wives of Windsor[Δ]

Measure for Measure[+]

The Comedy of Errors[+]

Much Ado About Nothing

Love's Labor's Lost

A Midsummer Night's Dream

The Merchant of Venice

As You Like It[+]

The Taming of the Shrew[+]

All's Well that Ends Well[+]

Twelfth Night, or What You Will[+]

The Winter's Tale[+]

## HISTORIES

King John[+]

Richard the Second

The First Part of Henry the Fourth

The Second Part of Henry the Fourth

Henry the Fifth[Δ]

The First Part of Henry the Sixth[+]

The Second Part of Henry the Sixth

The Third Part of Henry the Sixth

Richard the Third

Henry the Eighth[+]

## TRAGEDIES

Coriolanus[+]

Titus Andronicus

Romeo and Juliet[Δ]

Troilus and Cressida[*]

Timon of Athens[+]

Julius Caesar[+]

Macbeth[+]

Hamlet[Δ]

King Lear

Othello

Antony and Cleopatra[+]

Cymbeline[+]

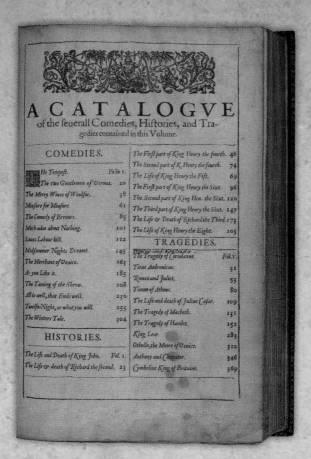

The "catalogue page" of the First Folio, aka the book's table of contents. Note that someone has written in a listing for *Troilus and Cressida* under "Tragedies." This was one of the lucky copies to include that play.

The image shows a catalogue page reading:

# A CATALOGVE
of the seuerall Comedies, Histories, and Tragedies contained in this Volume.

NOTE: The text for *Pericles* was not published in the First Folio, perhaps because the printers could not obtain the rights to reprint it. This play joined the collected works of Shakespeare in 1663 with the publication of the Third Folio.

+ The texts of these plays had not previously been published. They could easily have become lost and forgotten if not for their inclusion in the First Folio.

✱ *Troilus and Cressida* was added after some copies of the First Folio had already been sold; it was not listed in the book's table of contents.

Δ These titles have sometimes been called the bad quartos. Such pronouncements can seem like much ado about nothing, though, because some of the plays, such as *Hamlet*, had "good quartos" published while Shakespeare was still alive. And, as you've heard, maybe folks even liked the old "bad quartos" back then. Again, perhaps much ado about nothing. Let's just say, all's well that ends well.

# A NOTE FROM
# THE AUTHOR

On my second day of research at the Folger Shakespeare Library, a reference specialist named Abbie Weinberg informed me that she had something for me to see. On a nearby table she had placed a copy of the original quarto for *A Midsummer Night's Dream*. Beside it, and dwarfing it by all dimensions, sat a copy of the First Folio. Not a replica, an original First Folio, specifically the copy known as Folger First Folio 72.

It is a big book.

Even so, my first impression upon handling it was surprise. The volume is unexpectedly light considering its dimensions; it only weighs around three pounds. (In contrast, my replica of the First Folio, published in 1996, weighs more than seven pounds.) The original book's paper accounts for the difference, for its leaves are mere wisps of fibrous material. Despite their lightness, they imply durability, and Ms. Weinberg encouraged me to page through the volume.

I can hear you asking, "Did you wear protective gloves?" So, no, we did not. The Folger maintains that as long as your hands are clean you are less likely to damage the pages when your fingers can feel them. Gloves dull those sensations and can lead to accidents. As I turned the paper leaves I was able to observe the handwritten notes of early readers, stains from age and wear, watermarks embedded in various sheets, and, most of all, page after page of the plays of William Shakespeare.

Eric Rasmussen and Anthony James West identified this copy as number 130 in their 2012 *Descriptive Catalogue* of every known First Folio. They report that it was owned by two or more generations of barons from the Forester family of Shropshire, England. We know that Henry and Emily Folger bought the leather-bound book from a British book dealer in July 1926 for $41,000, a sum equivalent to about $700,000 today when adjusted for inflation. It was the couple's seventy-second purchase of a First Folio; hence the volume's name in their collection.

Rasmussen and West devoted three pages to their inventory of the copy's unique details. My own assessment of Folger 72/West 130 was far less clinical. It was in turns exciting, intimidating, fascinating, exhilarating, and overwhelming to be in the presence of this book. One does not think strategically around a First Folio, or at least I did not on that day. I lost all sense of time. I never felt rushed, but I could not have spent more than twenty minutes with Folger 72 and its diminutive companion before feeling ready to bid the volumes farewell. I thanked Ms. Weinberg and watched as she passed them to a colleague for their return to the vault located two floors below.

And then?

And then I realized that I could not just resume my review of Joseph Moxon's *Mechanick Exercises* from 1683 and Ben Jonson's *Workes* from 1616. I felt a strong urge to pause, to step out of doors, to reflect more fully upon what I had just experienced. As I passed through the swinging wooden doors that frame the Reading Room, I was surprised to discover that my reaction would include weeping. I had internalized so much joy, and exhilaration, and marvel that I could only express it through deep breaths and tears, the way one might sigh at the sight of a pleasing painting or cry at the sound of beautiful music.

But in this case, my tears celebrated a book.

# RESEARCH NOTES AND ACKNOWLEDGMENTS

This book began, appropriately enough, with a play, although it was not one written by William Shakespeare. I remain in the debt of Lauren Gunderson, playwright of *The Book of Will*, for introducing me to the story of the First Folio. I must simultaneously acknowledge my favorite company of actors, the American Players Theatre of Spring Green, Wisconsin, who staged an irresistible production of Ms. Gunderson's play during 2019. I attended the show three times in the space of a few weeks, driving nearly four hours round-trip on each occasion for the joy of the experience.

I already counted myself as something of a Shakespeare-aficionado, having known about and enjoyed his plays since, well, forever! But this First Folio business was a new twist for me. Could it actually be true? Was there really that much drama behind the gathering of so much drama? The more I learned, the more I wanted to know, and that curiosity took me before the year was out to the Folger Shakespeare Library in Washington, DC.

I must pause here to thank two librarians: Edith Ching, who is an instructor at the University of Maryland, and K. T. Horning, then the director of the Cooperative Children's Book Center at the University of Wisconsin–Madison. Each kindly vouched for me as a researcher worthy of admission to the Folger collections. It is entirely thanks to them that I was able to pass through the Reading Room's doors and enter another world.

Research and reference librarian Abbie Weinberg served as my guide from there. I appreciate the respect she and others accorded to me as an author of children's nonfiction with a brief academic pedigree who aspired to work alongside international scholars. While at the library, I had the pleasure of meeting staff member Melanie Leung; she kindly offered me a hands-on tutorial about seventeenth-century printing using the Folger's scaled replica press.

Although my experiences at the Folger were limited to the span of a week, they enriched my work for the duration of this project. In addition to this hands-on archival work, I read numerous books about Shakespeare's life, his literature, and the First Folio itself. The bibliography that follows is infused with my appreciation for each work and its creators. Throughout the process I drew on my love of Shakespeare's plays, his joy in language, and my delight in a lifetime of intersections with them both.

My parents, Dolores and Henry Bausum, deserve recognition for helping to spark my literary curiosity and publishing pursuits. Each of them wrote, edited, and published in their own right while encouraging me to do the same. My mother, a lifelong book lover who was in her nineties when I worked on this project, cheered me on tirelessly. My father, a historian who lived to greet his ninety-fifth year but not to see this work, nonetheless laid a path for me to the Folger. When I was just a girl and could barely grasp the meaning of research, he spent a summer immersed in the Folger collections. The place has held a reverential aura for me ever since. It was therefore beyond poignant to push past the same Reading Room doors that he would have opened a half century earlier and detect a hint of his lingering enthusiasm and presence inside.

Having written a book celebrating the making of an old book, it is particularly appropriate to celebrate the very modern team that has helped to bring this one into being. Hannah Mann, my agent at Writers House, believed in the project from first glance even though its text seemed to break all the rules of children's publishing. We weren't sure what it might become, but we knew that the right editor would, and that person turned out to be Catherine S. Frank, editor at large for Peachtree Publishing. Catherine coaxed all the right revisions out of the text and made it sing its unruly song with growing perfection. Under her guidance, *The Bard and the Book* found ideal collaborators for its production. Kerry Martin, the creative director for Peachtree, Holiday House, and Pixel+Ink, delivered a brilliant design for the book. She also recruited artist Marta Sevilla to serve as its illustrator. Together they have transformed my oddball manuscript into this stunning result. Thanks also to copy editor Barbara Perris and others who supported the production process.

Most of all, I am grateful to John Heminge, Henry Condell, Ralph Crane, Isaac Jaggard, William Jaggard, and the many others—even John Leason—who saved the plays of William Shakespeare from oblivion.

Endless thanks to one and all!

# THE MAKING OF
# THIS BOOK

Many hands around the globe and a variety of machines have helped to make this book. Despite the passage of time, the steps in that process share remarkable similarities—as well as some notable differences—with those behind the creation of the First Folio. Read on and see for yourself.

The original text for this book was composed electronically by the author at her home in Wisconsin using Microsoft Word. No backward letters required, thankfully! People in locations across the United States, including New York City, Atlanta, and New Orleans, helped the text become a book. Creative Director Kerry Martin converted the manuscript into printing fonts while designing the project, using such typefaces as Granjon, Crypt, and Cochin. Original illustrations were created by the illustrator, Marta Sevilla, at her studio in Madrid, Spain, using gouache and colored pencils for the cover and a digital medium for the inside of the book.

The colorful marbled-paper borders used throughout the book are photographic images similar to handmade sheets from the eighteenth and nineteenth centuries; they are reminiscent of materials used when copies of the First Folio received new bindings during that period. The original sheets were made by suspending various colors of ink on a liquid surface, gently combing or otherwise manipulating the colors into patterns, and then placing a sheet of paper on this surface to transfer the vibrant design.

The book was printed on a sheetfed press in DongGuan, China, using rolls of machine-made Oji Zunma paper produced in NanTong, China. After exiting the printing press the sheets were mechanically folded and gathered into coded bundles, which are now simply called signatures. (You know what those are!) This book is composed of 9 signatures, which were section sewn in 12 pages for 8 signatures and 16 pages for 1 signature for a total of 112 pages.

Human hands guided this and all other steps in the production process, with the publisher's director of production and manufacturing, Melanie McMahon Ives, coordinating all phases of the operation. Completed books were boxed and shipped by ocean freighter to distribution points in the United States and beyond. Publicists and marketing representatives have promoted interest in this book through social media, advertising, and one-on-one conversations with librarians and booksellers. Copies are being stocked with online retailers, storefront chains, and at independent bookshops reminiscent of those that sold the First Folio beginning in 1623 (but with a greater diversity of beverages and snacks).

One thing hasn't changed. When you open the book, you still turn the pages by hand (even if you are viewing it electronically), and enjoy its contents with your eyes. Doodling remains optional.

# CITATIONS FROM
# THE PLAYS OF
# WILLIAM SHAKESPEARE

"Devise, wit; write, pen: for I am for whole volumes in folio."
—*Love's Labor's Lost*, Act I, Scene 2, lines 164–165 (*The Norton Shakespeare*, third edition, 819).

"All the world's a stage . . ."
—*As You Like It*, Act II, Scene 7, lines 139–142 (*The Norton Shakespeare*, third edition, 1648).

"This wooden O."
—*Henry the Fifth*, Prologue, line 13 (*The Norton Shakespeare*, third edition, 1545).

"To be or not to be: that is the question."
—*Hamlet*, Act III, Scene 1, line 55 (*The Norton Shakespeare*, third edition, 1802).

"Blow wind and crack your cheeks!"
—*King Lear*, Act III, Scene 2, line 1 (*The Norton Shakespeare*, third edition, 2408).

"A horse, a horse, my kingdom for a horse!"
—*Richard the Third*, Act V, Scene 4, line 7 (*The Norton Shakespeare*, third edition, 645).

"Parting is such sweet sorrow."
—*Romeo and Juliet*, Act II, Scene 2, line 226 (*The Norton Shakespeare*, third edition, 990).

"Were it not better . . ."
—*As You Like It*, Act I, Scene 3, lines 110–112 (*The Norton Shakespeare*, third edition, 1637).

"If it live in your memory, begin at this line . . ."
—*Hamlet*, Act II, Scene 2, lines 370–371 (*The Norton Shakespeare*, third edition, 1797).

**"To be, or not to be—ay, there's the point."**
—*Hamlet*, Scene 7, line 114 (citing First Quarto from 1603 in *The Norton Shakespeare*, third edition, 1875).

**"Double, double, toil and trouble . . ."**
—*Macbeth*, Act IV, Scene 1, lines 10–11 (*The Norton Shakespeare*, third edition, 2753).

**"A glooming peace this morning with it brings . . ."**
—*Romeo and Juliet*, Act V, Scene 3, lines 305–306 (*The Norton Shakespeare*, third edition, 1035).

**"pursued by a bear."**
—*The Winter's Tale*, Act III, Scene 3, line 57 (*The Norton Shakespeare*, third edition, 3165).

**"The poore Sonle set sining, by a Sicamour tree."**
—*Othello*, Act IV, Scene 3, Folger First Folio 47, per Blayney (1991), 16–17.

**"The poore Soule sat singing, by a Sicamour tree."**
—*Othello*, Act IV, Scene 3 (marked as line 3011, *The Norton Facsimile*, 841).

**"Sometime a horse I'll be, sometime a hound . . ."**
—*A Midsummer Night's Dream*, Act III, Scene 1, lines 96–97 (*The Norton Shakespeare*, third edition, 1067).

**"Oh, wonderful, wonderful, and most wonderful . . ."**
—*As You Like It,* Act III, Scene 2, lines 175–177 (*The Norton Shakespeare,* third edition, 1654).

**"Juliet and her Romeo."**
—*Romeo and Juliet*, Act V, Scene 3, line 310 (*The Norton Shakespeare*, third edition, 1035).

**"O thou monster, Ignorance, how deformed dost thou look! . . ."**
—*Love's Labor's Lost*, Act IV, Scene 2, lines 20–23 (*The Norton Shakespeare*, third edition, 834).

# SOURCE NOTES

## PROLOGUE

**Actually Shakespeare may not . . . :** Cooper, 57; National Portrait Gallery.

## —ACT I—
## WILLIAM SHAKESPEARE BECOMES BRILLIANT, THEN DIES

**In 1564, William Shakespeare made his entrance . . . :** Greenblatt (2004), 161, 166, 330–331, 378–379; Orlin, 102, 121.

**And London filled his purse . . . :** Greenblatt (2004), 149–150, 189, 210, 291–293; Greenblatt et al. (2016), 27; Smith (2015), 135–136.

**As a playwright, Shakespeare would . . . :** Greenblatt (2004), 294–295; Greenblatt et al. (2016), 112; Smith (2015), 124; Thompson and Taylor, 82.

**Shakespeare didn't just write parts willy-nilly . . . :** Greenblatt et al. (2016), 109, 1166; Smith (2015), 103–107.

**And what about the leading ladies? . . . :** Maguire and Smith, 164–167.

**There is this thing called aging . . . :** Greenblatt (2004), 144, 387; Greenblatt et al. (2016), 387; Smith (2015), 136.

## —ACT II—
## THE FLEETING NATURE OF THEATER PREPARES TO VANQUISH MACBETH

**When Richard Burbage created the role . . . :** Blayney (1991), 1; Collins, 24; Greenblatt (2004), 194, 291; Greenblatt et al. (2016), 69, 2,709.

**The bad quartos . . . :** Blayney (1991), 1; Greenblatt et al. (2016), 76–77, 1760; Smith (2015), 20; Thompson and Taylor, 86.

**"Pray tell me Ben . . . :"** Blayney (1991), 1; Collins, 26.

**Heminge and Condell, plus the Jaggards and . . . :** Blayney (1991), 2–3, 9.

**These gathered sheets were known as a quire . . . :** Blayney (1991), 9; Collins, 24–25; Greenblatt et al. (2016), 77–78.

**Alas, page numbers weren't particularly helpful . . . :** Blayney (1996), xxxv–xxxvii; Smith (2015), 141–143, 157. Pagination details taken from Hinman, *The Norton Facsimile* (1996).

# —ACT III—
# ROMEO AND JULIET
# TUSSLE WITH THEIR FIRST TEEN READER

**And there were the quartos—the good quartos . . . :** Blayney (1991), 1; Greenblatt (2004), 380; Mays, 28.

**These acts worked like chapters . . . :** Blayney, (1991), 9; Hirsh, 227; Smith (2015), 38, 146, 149.

**It took about three hundred years . . . :** Blayney (1991), 9–10; Blayney (1996), xxxiii–xxxiv; Walkling.

**Each compositor worked from their own . . . :** Blayney (1991), 10–11; Smith (2015), 147.

**Which brings us to Compositor E . . . :** Blayney (1991), 11; Collins, 167–168; Smith (2015), 120.

**Scholars have calculated that compositors had to set . . . :** Blayney (1991), 18; Smith (2015), 122; Moxon (Vol. II), 351–354; Smith (2016), 1.

# —ACT IV—
# SHAKESPEARE CATCHES FIRE, LITERALLY

**Amazingly, we think we know who purchased . . . :** Smith (2016), 2–4, 7–8.

**Literary scholars have speculated for some time . . . :** Blayney (1991), 2; Collins 153–155; Folger Shakespeare Library, "Meet the Folger First Folios" and "Folger First Folio 1"; Smith (2015), 158; West (2003), 176.

**The Golden Retriever Folio . . . :** Flaim; Folger Shakespeare Library, "Folger First Folio 19."

**Copies of the original edition . . . :** Thomas Pennant Barton Collection; Blayney (1991), 9; Collins, 109, 138–139, 235; Folger Shakespeare Library, "About the Folger First Folios"; Orlin, 12–13; West (2003), 186–187.

**Today the most coveted edition . . . :** Mays, 57–59; Smith (2015), 25.

**Countless copies of the first three . . . :** Mays, 25, 59–61; West (2003), 186–187.

# —ACT V—
# THE WORLD GOES NUTS
# FOR SHAKESPEARE

**Around the turn of the last century . . . :** Collins, 125–127; Mays, 110, 166, 330; Rasmussen and West, xi; Smith (2016), 31; West (2001), 135.

**Two years later they confirmed the discovery . . . :** Coughlan; Folger Shakespeare Library, "A New First Folio Discovery"; Ford; Lewis; Morris, "Found in Warwickshire" and "Shakespeare in France"; Schuessler.

**What we do know is the whereabouts . . . :** Blayney (1991), 42; Folger Shakespeare Library, "About the Folger First Folios," "The Collection," and "What Is a First Folio?"; Folio400, "First Folios around the Globe"; Mays, 209–211, 265; Rasmussen and West, 868–872; Weinberg and DeBold.

**Very few people possess their own copy of this book . . . :** Folger Shakespeare Library, Folger First Folio 36; Mays, 241; Heather Wolfe.

# BACK MATTER

**Contents of the First Folio:** Blayney (1991), 17; Smith (2015), 14.

**A Note from the Author:** Folger Shakespeare Library, "Folger First Folio 72"; Mays, 223, 320; Rasmussen and West, 524–526; Weinberg.

**The Making of THIS Book:** Richard J. Wolfe, 1–3, 63, 73, 147.

First Folio, a rare copy with its original calf leather binding still intact.

# BIBLIOGRAPHY

All websites accessed 8/30/2023.

Thomas Pennant Barton Collection, Boston Public Library. https://www.bpl.org/archival_subject/performing-arts/.

Blayney, Peter W. M. *The First Folio of Shakespeare* (exhibition catalog). The Folger Shakespeare Library, 1991.

_____. "Introduction to the Second Edition," *The Norton Facsimile: The First Folio of Shakespeare*. W. W. Norton & Company, 1996.

Collins, Paul. *The Book of William: How Shakespeare's First Folio Conquered the World*. Bloomsbury, 2009.

Cooper, Tarnya, with essays by Marcia Pointon, James Shapiro, and Stanley Wells. *Searching for Shakespeare*. Yale University Press, 2006.

Coughlan, Sean. "Shakespeare First Folio discovered on Scottish island." BBC News, April 7, 2016. https://www.bbc.com/news/education-35973094.

Flaim, Denise. "Golden Retriever History: Behind the Breed's 'Unfashionable' Past." American Kennel Club, July 1, 2020. https://www.akc.org/expert-advice/dog-breeds/behind-the-breed-golden-retriever-history/.

Folger Shakespeare Library. "About the Folger First Folios." https://www.folger.edu/shakespeare/first-folio/about-folger-folios.

_____. "Collection Highlights." https://www.folger.edu/explore/collection-highlights.

_____. "Folger First Folio 1." https://www.folger.edu/folger-first-folio-number-1.

_____. "Folger First Folio 19." https://www.folger.edu/first-folio-number-19.

_____. "Folger First Folio 36." https://www.folger.edu/first-folio-number-36.

_____. "Folger First Folio 72." https://www.folger.edu/first-folio-number-72.

_____. "About the Folger First Folios." https://www.folger.edu/shakespeare/first-folio/meet-folger-folios.

_____. "A New First Folio Discovery" (undated interview). https://www.folger.edu/shakespeare-unlimited/first-folio-discovery-france.

_____. "What Is a First Folio?" (FAQ). https://www.folger.edu/shakespeare/first-folio/faq.

Folio400. "First Folios around the Globe." https://folio400.com/where-are-they/.

Ford, Margaret. "The Schuckburgh Folio at the Globe." Folio400, April 23, 2016. https://folio400.com/phernalia/the-shuckburgh-folio-at-the-globe/.

Greenblatt, Stephen, general editor, with Walter Cohen, Suzanne Gossett, Jean E. Howard, Katharine Eisamin Maus, and Gordon McMullan. *The Norton Shakespeare, Third Edition*. W. W. Norton & Company, 2016.

Greenblatt, Stephen. *Will in the World*. W. W. Norton & Company, 2004.

Hinman, Charlton, preparer. *The Norton Facsimile: The First Folio of Shakespeare*. W. W. Norton & Company, second edition, 1996.

Hirsh, James. "Act Divisions in the Shakespeare First Folio." *The Papers of the Bibliographical Society of America*, Vol. 96, No. 2 (June 2002), pp. 219–256.

Lewis, Danny. "A New Copy of Shakespeare's First Folio Was Found in a Scottish Library." *Smithsonian Magazine*, April 7, 2016. https://www.smithsonianmag.com/smart-news/new-copy-shakespeares-first-folio-was-found-scottish-library-180958694/.

Maguire, Laurie, and Emma Smith. *30 Great Myths About Shakespeare*. John Wiley & Sons, 2013.

Mays, Andrea. *The Millionaire and the Bard: Henry Folger's Obsessive Hunt for Shakespeare's First Folio*. Simon & Schuster (paperback edition), 2016.

Morris, Sylvia. "Found in Warwickshire: the Schuckburg folios." The Shakespeare blog, March 24, 2016. http://theshakespeareblog.com/2016/03/found-in-warwickshire-the-shuckburgh-folios/.

_____. "Shakespeare in France: the St Omer First Folio." The Shakespeare blog, Dec. 1, 2014. http://theshakespeareblog.com/2014/12/shakespeare-in-france-the-st-omer-first-folio/.

Moxon, Joseph. *Mechanick Exercises: Or the Doctrine of Handy-works Applied to the Art of Printing* (Vols. I and II). London, 1683.
    (Vol. I) https://library.si.edu/digital-library/book/moxonsmechanicke11896moxo
    (Vol. II) https://library.si.edu/digital-library/book/moxonsmechan-icke21683moxo

National Portrait Gallery [United Kingdom], "Searching for Shakespeare." https://www.npg.org.uk/whatson/exhibitions/2006/searching-for-shakespeare.php.

Orlin, Lena Cowen. *The Private Life of William Shakespeare*. Oxford University Press, 2021.

Rasmussen, Eric. *The Shakespeare Thefts: In Search of the First Folios*. Palgrave Macmillan, 2011.

Rasmussen, Eric, and Anthony James West. *The Shakespeare First Folios: A Descriptive Catalogue*. Palgrave Macmillan, 2012.

Raymond, Joad. *Pamphlets and Pamphleteering in Early Modern Britain*. Cambridge University Press, 2003.

Schuessler, Jennifer. "Shakespeare Folio Discovered in France." *New York Times*, Nov. 25, 2014. https://www.nytimes.com/2014/11/26/arts/shakespeare-folio-discovered-in-france-.html.

Smith, Emma. *The Making of Shakespeare's First Folio*. Bodleian Library, University of Oxford, 2015.

_____. *Shakespeare's First Folio: Four Centuries of an Iconic Book*. Oxford University Press, 2016.

Thompson, Ann, and Neil Taylor. *Hamlet* (Arden Shakespeare), Bloomsbury, 2016 (revised edition).

U.S. Bureau of Labor Statistics inflation calculator (data cited in text is current as of October 2022). https://data.bls.gov/cgi-bin/cpicalc.pl.

Walkling, Andrew R. "Hinman, Redux." *The Collation*, Folger Shakespeare Library, May 10, 2018. https://collation.folger.edu/2018/05/hinman-redux/.

Weinberg, Abbie, research and reference librarian, Folger Shakespeare Library. Email correspondence with the author, April 26, 2021.

_____, and Elizabeth DeBold. "The Other First Folio." *The Collation*, Folger Shakespeare Library, Oct. 11, 2016. https://collation.folger.edu/2016/10/the-other-first-folio/.

West, Anthony James. *The Shakespeare First Folio: The History of the Book* (Volume I). Oxford University Press, 2001.

_____. *The Shakespeare First Folio: The History of the Book* (Volume II). Oxford University Press, 2003.

Wolfe, Heather. "Scissors inside books?" *The Collation*, Folger Shakespeare Library, Dec. 6, 2016. https://collation.folger.edu/2016/12/scissors-inside-books/.

Wolfe, Richard J. *Marbled Paper: Its History, Techniques, and Patterns*. University of Pennsylvania Press, 1990.

# ADDITIONAL RESOURCES

All websites accessed 8/31/2023.

American Players Theatre
https://americanplayers.org/
The author's home away from home for Shakespeare and more, nestled in the woods near Spring Green, Wisconsin.

The Bodleian First Folio
https://firstfolio.bodleian.ox.ac.uk/
A digital facsimile of a First Folio copy from the Bodleian Library, Oxford, England.

Do-it-yourself First Folio and Virtual Printing House
https://www.folger.edu/shakespeare/first-folio/diy-first-folio
A hands-on virtual workshop where users organize sheets for printing quires.

The First Folio at the Folger
https://www.folger.edu/shakespeare/first-folio
The history, the book, and other resources from the Folger Shakespeare Library.

Folger Shakespeare Library
https://www.folger.edu/
As conceived by Henry and Emily Folger and dedicated in 1932 in Washington, DC.

Folio400
https://folio400.com/
Celebrating the history of the First Folio and its 400th birthday in 2023.

The Royal Shakespeare Company
https://www.rsc.org.uk/shakespeare
The Bard's hometown stage, established in 1875 at Stratford-upon-Avon, England.

Shakespeare at the Folger
https://www.folger.edu/explore/shakespeares-life/
A gateway to all things Shakespeare and more through the Folger Shakespeare Library.

Shakespeare's Globe
https://www.shakespearesglobe.com/
Inspired by the original, this replica theater sits on the banks of the Thames in London, just where it ought to be.

William Shakespeare's Complete Works
http://shakespeare.mit.edu/
The first digitized archive of Shakespeare's plays and poetry, courtesy of Massachusetts Institute of Technology, Cambridge, Massachusetts.

# PHOTO CREDITS

Folger Shakespeare Library:
6–7: GA795.L6 V5 1625 Cage, image 115255
14: STC 22273 Fo.1 no.12, image 119364
23: PR2752 1861-1871 Sh.Col., image 2346
35: STC 22273 Fo.1 no.05, image 5333
44: ART Vol. f81 no.4, image 3023
60: STC 22273 Fo.1 no.72, image 51109
62: R1876, image 12953
68: STC 22273 Fo.1 no.78, image 6405
71: photo by Julie Ainsworth, image 54568
79: STC 22273 Fo.1 no.08, image 126834
93: STC 22273 Fo.1 no.30, image 153655

© National Portrait Gallery, London:
viii

# INDEX

*Italic* page numbers refer to illustrations.

# ABOUT THE
# CREATORS

Sam Boutelle

**ANN BAUSUM** writes about history for readers of all ages from her home in southern Wisconsin. Her books frequently explore issues of social justice, including women's voting rights, the Civil Rights Movement of the American South, free speech, immigration, and queer history.

Her titles appear frequently on lists of recommended and notable books and have received numerous awards. The body of her work has been recognized nationally by the Children's Book Guild of Washington, DC. Find out more about her work at *AnnBausum.com*.

Mario Triguero

**MARTA SEVILLA** is an illustrator and creative based in Madrid, Spain. Her work focuses on editorial illustration, children's books, book covers, posters, and surface design. Her illustrations are colorful, quirky, and humorous. She works from her illustration studio, creating art for clients around the world. Visit her at *MartaSevilla.es*.

FINIS.